FALSE SPRING

FALSE / SPRING

poems

DARREN / BIFFORD

BRICK BOOKS

LIBRARY AND ARCHIVES CANADA CATALOGUING IN PUBLICATION

Bifford, Darren, 1977–, author
False spring / Darren Bifford.
Poems.
Issued in print and electronic formats.
ISBN 978-1-77131-476-3 (softcover).
ISBN 978-1-77131-478-7 (pdf).
ISBN 978-1-77131-477-0 (epub)
I. Title.
PS8603.I383F35 2018   C811'.6   C2017-907253-6   C2017-907254-4

We acknowledge the Government of Canada, the Canada Council for the Arts, and the Ontario Arts Council for their support of our publishing program.

Author photo by the Government of Canada.
The book is set in Quant by Hoftype.
Design and layout by Natalie Olsen, Kisscut Design.
Printed and bound by Coach House Printing.

BRICK BOOKS
431 Boler Road, Box 20081
London, Ontario N6K 4G6
www.brickbooks.ca

Here it seemed customary to sit with your elbows propped up and your fists pressed against your temples; Karl could not help thinking of his Latin teacher...

FRANZ KAFKA, from *Amerika*

CONTENTS

II

III

LETTER OF INTENT

Somehow the end comes nearer when you're not looking.

To dissolve all problems would mean a clearer way of living into the future.

I for one desire those very bright and well-positioned days bequeathed to baby boomers.

When you're not looking is when it's commonly said the end comes nearer.

Uncommonly, it's said: exactly when you're looking it arrives, which is a real issue.

However well everything seems to be going, you attend also to the darkening sky.

The Pixies' "Stormy Weather" is an end-of-the-party sing-a-long track for my generation.

In my own life and in the lives of my friends is the way I begin my sentences.

The end comes knocking, as in the joke.

Unlike the joke, it doesn't knock.

Does the weather mirror the soul or Vice Versa?

By Vice Versa I mean the pub in Montreal.

I can't breathe when the sky turns black, which suggests the priority of the weather.

Physiological changes precede the insights that might result in new therapies or pills.

I'm off topic, however. However else you might put the essential matter.

The spirit of the thing, I mean.

I wish it were the great age of rereading but that is simply how it is for me.

May I take a number, you a prescription?

Sell me something. My hopes are very great.

I

I get the precedents
but not the thing by its face.
How I speak with a voice
its voice would erase.

THE BIRTH OF REVOLUTIONARY DESIRE

When Hiero descended into those old word-
Worlds I stayed awake all night; what would
Be in contrary circumstances a bloodbath looks
For us a lot like getting along as well as we can.
Now everything worth doing takes longer than
Before. To despair that things in general would
Be better if one simply stopped being
Around—is from Hiero's point of view *a small-
Scale worry*, the likes of which are easy to feel
Nostalgic about. O Christ don't go getting Hiero
Sidetracked. His temptations are not Satan's
Sweet nothings and his uh-uh's are not so simply
Uttered. His character does little to protect his heart.
It's all on the table, as if a table. Hiero says
The bad cough I can't kick was picked up in 1789.
A revolution made to fit helium-inflated nouns,
Occupying wide open spaces, filled the blue
Sky with floating white balloons. Of course,
Of course they will say rivers burned through the night;
That the women all wailed, their children sold.

OF FIRST AND LAST THINGS

Do you recall when, late in the film *Time Bandits*,
The adventurers collided with an invisible wall?
They smacked against their world's limit, against
The limit of all possible worlds, suddenly arrested
Not by the end of time but that of space.
In the wall's illusion, the transparence of further
Country, more wandering in and out of history.
They shattered the wall as if it were made of glass,
Threw a rock against its side: it collapsed,
Revealing the backstage of a bad game-show set,
Where visible chunks of evil like molten rock
Glowed red and smoked on the floor. The stage
Show finished but for a janitor's work
Sweeping up the debris. For the small bandits
History opened and closed like the doors of a house
Into which they sneaked and stole civilization's loot.
Unmoored from untruth, those free spirits, unaware
Of what appears later on, a jackhammer of black boots.

THE GREAT BEAST

In the middle distance the courtier of bulls
Dances for a vast hidden crowd, a crowd unrepresented
Except by the painting's pitch-black backdrop
In which we infer their presence and infer
How the heat is palpable, how the dust eddied
By the wind whirls into itself and into the hands
Of children for whom these displays of violence
Later return in their dreams as coal-fleshed
Miners return home changed by the labour
Of their days. I do not wish any of this. That's
Just the thing, isn't it? One bull already dead,
The other dying, and each will remain poised
Thus in the middle distance as if outside of time.
Icy snow pelts my window; I turn my head that way.

THE ETYMOLOGY OF IDEOLOGY

They didn't know what they were doing. The train
Tracks on the hills behind their minuscule town were long
Abandoned; the last train had passed through years before.
So the body they found, the horses near the pastures,
The dogs unleashed in fields, all this took on its own
Larger contour, like a collective vocation, an invisible
Order into the late afternoon, the hours before stray parents
Called one another and inquired into their children's
Whereabouts. I have not seen them at all, not for a long
Time. Up in the bush the fires begin intentionally. Because
The hero of the story, the smallest, is bored too easily. Or
Because—it's anyone's guess, really—he is already insane.

ARCHAIC TORSO

We cannot know his ordinary head
except from photographs, eyes wholly terrified.
And yet his torso, bent over his bound hands,
is like a light flickering in an empty apartment,

illuminating: a table, some glass, itself. Otherwise
he'd be merely bare life, unlucky in foreign lands,
a common captured adventurer, hostage
to barbarians in a bombed city, almost a fiction.

Otherwise you could forget him. His body,
beneath vacant space, poised before collapse,
would not hesitate, tremble as if a living man:

he would not, from all the borders of his headless corpse,
burst like a dumb star: for there is no place left
where you aren't seen. Your life will change.

FALSE SPRING IS THE NEW THING

The first spring is always false. They call
It that because everyone wishes further
Hibernation. There's a town the existence
Of which I learnt when I was a child: all its
Inhabitants sleep as much of the day and night
As is possible. It's a *thing* to arrive into
Their public square unannounced.
My one practice is to summon indifference
To the most consequential events: what's left
Of the Great Barrier Reef, for instance; the situation
In Syria; my brother's long illness. I wish for a say
In what qualifies as an externality. That woman
In Toronto who, when asked about the last
Federal election, responded, *I don't know
What that means.* The guy next door
With that fucking dog, for instance. Or Mark, who sits
Outside the liquor store, hat in hand, all spring,
Reading. Do I care what he's reading? Not all hope
Is great hope, even given this as-if spring.
I've also felt the desire to join the slumber
Of that hidden town behind the mountains.
The kid who made it there came not without
His own questions. As for answers, what seemed
To him like reasons were little better than a roll
Of the dice, a yes and a no and a no and a no.

STAY

Check, now stop. The inroads are closed.
No further progress is possible. Hold on.
The stay is temporary; all judgment postponed
Until a new language is learned. A song
May also work. My stomach hurts.
Stay here until I return but I will not return.
Any decision is also temporary although the situation
May well be regarded as permanent. Wait.
Stay until the strike is over. Look at all the miners
Returning forever on a beat-up road
Through no one's Heaven. All their action
Stayed: their speech, tar-song. But how
They show endurance! Is it out of habit
That we stay here, hanging around exactly as if
We don't know what else to do? Who's
Giving the orders? I'll stay standing, stiff. And that
Sharp pitch heard first by the dogs?—I hear it next.

THE ELEMENTS OF COHESION MUST BE WEAKENED
Mark 5: 9 - 13

In the Gospels demons hurl themselves headlong
Into a herd of swine and the swine promptly rush
Over a cliff and drown in the sea. It is easily a scene
Goya imagines quite closely in another context:
When revolutionaries in the hours before dawn, sleepless
For several nights, walk now closely together, as if
Synchronized after a long-rehearsed performance,
And prepare to execute two brothers. A two-year-old's
Tantrum likewise is always preceded by a trespass
Into a country of endless exhaustion. No one present
Notices how he passes over that border. Soon he trips
And slips out of his mind, screaming and convulsing.
His eyes evidence a faraway look. Cities are bombed out
Beneath them. Outside the tombs the demons
Press the heads of two men into their own hands.
Nearby, the smell of swine. With Goya it is the same:
Innocent bystanders hide their faces behind their hands
As in a game of peekaboo. Recall how in Kurosawa's *Dreams*,
When over the decimated landscape of the hills demons wail,
It's because their pain is too much: sharp bones protrude
Through their skulls. In Goya's painting we cannot see the eyes
Of the revolutionaries who will do the shooting. Their backs
Are turned, their heads are cocked low to the butts of their rifles.
We see how the surviving brother pleads. And we see how the one
Holding him steady stares out of his skull as if he will never sleep again.
I can see the city roofs and the spire of a church over low hills.
Beneath the cliffs, which are not visible, the sea is inaudible.
Perhaps Christ is about. Who knows! Goya's painting hangs
Close by on my wall. The revolutionaries locked in step, eyes unshut.

WHILE GREAT NATIONS RECAST
EVEN GREATER NATIONS RUSH IN

You're next in line. No less than a complete reversal
Will turn your scope toward the stars. How close the stars
When you wish someone would take your place among them.
Now failure triggers unaccountable depths in a ditch
Just this side of rifle and rattle; a little girl's curls cut
To size; the luxury of eating supper alone in silence
When no one cares to call out your name—I mean
Mine. Even though I know how that which happened
Happened, I'm still in the dark about why it happened at all.
By accident everyone arrived and shot their fireworks
On my shore? Or was it by design? Here is one hand,
Here is another. This I know for sure. Hitched to one
Another's arms, we spin around each other. A painter
Later imagines the remainder of the events that follow,
Namely my capture and release. The birth of my children.
The situation was tight while it lasted. It lasted like forever.

ON THE ORIGINS OF UTOPIA

Many people have long felt the desire to do something
With their lives besides consuming goods. They desire
To interact and develop but for this there is no remedy
Calculable in classical economics. This gets me
Wondering. It would be a fine thing, all that flourishing,
Along with everyone else, but also decently private
So as not to burden one's neighbours with too much noise
Or such a torrent of dumb ideas all at once. Requisite space
Is also allocated into the general scheme of the better life,
If not the best life, since the latter wedges its dissatisfaction
Into the minds of each of us according to our old desires,
Childhood vistas, incurable heartbreak by the age of sixteen.
It was silly then but also so totally serious that now our leaders
Wage their private warfare, their revenge, and we're all implicated.

THE FAILURE OF THE INTERNATIONAL SYSTEM

The dead horse later is not dead. The conquistador
Forgotten by his thirtieth year is resurrected
Into the fame of his youth. The staggered bull returns
To its stable of shit and hay, lies sickened there.
The Nuremberg crowds no more fail their individual
Intentions; they stay standing through the night and into
The next night. It's easy this way to remain happy.
Tomorrow we'll have never met one another; we'll
Have never married. Commonplace truths complicated
By new experience will take on again an adolescent glow.
When the dusk gave out its free anxieties to students
Living alone, there was no liquor to succour the hurt
And you stayed awake and listened to a single record,
Feared its repetition. Wished for finality like a switch.

ON TYRANNY

Such hateful things. Hiero and Simonides,
Reclining through the uninterrupted afternoon,
Contend that the tyrant cannot do better
Than immediately hanging himself. This is not bad advice
Except for the tyrant's refusal to listen to Hiero and Simonides,
Who've fled together into Goya's painting, *The Shooting of the Third
    of May*.
But they fail to outrun the tyrant's many admirers —
Those armed men, bored silly, lonely, who otherwise have nothing
    to do.
Now they're occupied with the At-Oneness of the tyrant's intentions:
The execution of Hiero and his friend, the poet, Simonides, dying
    beside him.
Still, Hiero does not cease to give his two-cents worth; he raises his
    arms;
If the blood-muck pooling beside his feet became a common fire
Around which those who were lonely told stories,
Then this would be Hiero's final story before the end of all that is
    Hiero:
Thus he stands and raises his arms above the earth, his gestures
The size of cosmos, his complaints Promethean —
Against fickle gods, against the machinery of lust,
A Tyrant's boredom, against those whose bodies
Are equal to mass times distance, whose ignorance
Is dense as a failed universe, whose hopes are dismantled
Like the station wagon of a family shot dead, in cold blood,
Ill-favoured and forgotten — Hiero sees it all,
Claims the remainder for the Greatest Story Ever Told,

The incredible bulk of a husband's failure; the noblest
Scholar on his hands and knees barks on command,
While furtive urchins run towards the river,
Lie on the ground, cover their bodies in mud, turn into slugs.
Now Hiero sees it all so quickly, he wants to tell it all,
But he vomits as he commences — with what great fortitude! —
To utter his final dispatched breath. Such hateful things.

LOOSE TEXTURE OF A COLLAPSING ORDER

Disregard the entirety of the preceding.
Of all your childhood nighttime terrors
select the recurring episode

wherein you could not open your eyes.
Scraps of sunlight scrape brilliantly by the remainder
of nature. Stone stars crowd in.

Cassandra, O you, little pieces of your voice
go unaccompanied by the violin, litter cold dry grass.
Growing out of apple trees, the limbs of a thin-limbed woman. So far

from evincing sympathy, away from their bodies,
so far under the dirt that all light dissipates, small civilizations
gawk up, and beside themselves, and behind themselves.

NOTES FROM A RECLUSIVE SCHOLAR

As for Orpheus's head: when the river god
Dived under the ground and took with him
The river, all its fish gasped and flipped out,
Choking on the air, their lungs wasps'
Hives: but where Orpheus's head lay open
On the rocks, gaping like a gutted fish,
I heard a song suspended in the open air,
Like that sense of rain before the rain. Is this life
Like a disease? Do we get another chance?
The singing head recalls the aftermath,
A child washed up on a beach in strange land.
Inside the temple of Apollo we flick away flies.

OCCUPATIONS

Whenever the dead are talking some poet
or another claims that he or she is listening
to what they're selling. What indeed is for sale
that I might buy with what I've livingly available?

It's like there's a small animal chewing the world
through my body, which is also the world, sort of.

In *Annie Hall*, Woody Allen
and the very great Diane Keaton
run into each other and have an awkward lunch:
the poets and the dead are like that.

It's a matter of how you say things and to whom.
We had all that love or what we called living around
one another, and now we're walking in a different light.

If the shades want so badly to talk, ask them what more
they have to say and whether it's really *that* important.
We're busy here. I know, I know, not fundamentally busy.
But the day is happening around us; it's all we've got.

THIS SUNSET LASTS FOREVER

There must have been a lot of beauty
At the end of empire. Scratch that.
Strictly the usual amount,
More or less, like in a movie
When before he is shot
The soldier considers the dewy grass or the dawn
Over yon golden hills. Which is to say
I doubt it. *Consider the fowls of the air and beasts of the field,*
Christ did *not* say on the Cross. *Why, why, why, why, why, why?*
Is closer to the mark. And it was no ordinary day
For those who were otherwise occupied with their lives,
Even given the torturer's horse scratching its innocent behind on a tree.
For there was a breaking sound in the sky;
We were all as terrified as other slow-witted animals, desirous and hungry.
I'm not getting over this in record time. *Oh my heavenly days*
Is what my grandmother sighed. Now which book will I take?
Will there be a record player? A mistake in these matters
Will commit us to eternal boredom. Help me
With a Jackson Pollock from the MoMA. His paintings,
In lieu of small fires or snowstorms, will serve to increase our contemplative
Capacity. Now if only we could get some help—I mean,
Help with the moving, not the moaning.
I've heard no pianos are housed on the isles of the blessed
Though the wind plays the trees and the trees are willing.
Now that my will is broken I am either left for dead
Or I shall see them forever, my wife, my little boy. They are crossing
Rue St-Denis on a winter afternoon, holding hands. Flaring in the mind
Awhile longer like a flare shot to the height from which it falls in the night sky,
Tumbling into wine-dark oceans,
We went down to the ship—

THE SCENE FROM HERE

So I see near the beach beside the docked
and decommissioned ferry, a makeshift flagpole
on which hangs, half-mast, the French *Tricolore*.

I run past. The route I take follows
the trail beside the channel, its slow waters
flowing from lake to lake, its currents shallow,

benign, so that no danger troubles the swimmers
who recline and drink on their rubber floats before
they leap in and submerge. Nothing is hidden of summer

in the valley where all along the shore
children build tiny sand castles, dig twisting moats
into the mud. Lone suckers feed on the lake floor.

It's been a weird July. Every afternoon for over a week
storms have broken over the mountains—lightning, thunder—
the rain falling hard. Conversation turns to the weather.

What's the worst they've seen (if they've seen it before)
those who've been here a long time can't recall
or won't say, and the weather anyhow has its own way

of doing things. It's easy to stare at the hills and think
about nothing. As if the mountains would have you wander
into them, burrow into fallen pine needles, stay there.

Soon I turn from the trail and run uphill on the old track
or where the railroad tracks were, the ones that once ran the span
of the valley from the coast into Alberta. History marks

landscape like a scar, like the flesh healed into woven stitches
above my right eye, so that a reddened furrow is cut close,
hardly visible except to those women who've pressed

their fingers there. In the evenings I'm reading Euripides
on my mother's patio, near the lakeshore where a giant peach
is open until late; teenage girls inside serving ice cream floats

later flutter about the beach above the glow of their cellphones.
Early in the morning last week I woke to the sound of a voice
announcing on a megaphone the names of marathon runners

as they crossed the finish line. AC/DC's "Thunderstruck," applause,
all the spent athletes like in Ovid, that story near the end
about the runner who had escaped the finale of the last age,

when iron returned to fire and fire to sand. He moved like an ant
below the gods who at that point were left with little to do;
they say Apollo caught him easily, pressed him between his finger

and thumb, squished and ground him up until he too was sand,
and flicked him down to where he was left with the rest of civilization,
subject to the wind's shifts. In the afternoon my three-year-old son

learns to swim. I prop him on my knees in the lake, cup my hands
underneath his arms; he does not let me relax my grip but screams
delight and terror when I throw him into the air and let him fall

again into my hands and collapse into my arms, cold
water splashing over his face and hair. He cries because water
is in his eyes and complains that it got into his mouth.

Later, on the sand, he tells me, *Babi, you protect me*. The truth
of what he says, that total trust, turns my heart transparent.
He is a diamond cut into the air. Midway, my run inclines to dust-

dry ponderosa bluffs, the shelter of my ear like caves carved into the clay
cliffs which rise here on either side, the trail metamorphosed into scree.
The Trojan Women all wail and wail. There is no happy conclusion.

The ships on which they sail take them elsewhere far away.
Last week in Nice a few young drunk Brits took selfies next to a family
mourning their dead. Life returns to normal quickly.

Out on the lake the boats pull skiers; above the water a man
harnessed to a parachute is pulled around awhile. The scene
from here shows him minuscule, like a dead man in an airborne pulley.

What is normal? The air I breathe is dry, dry. The mountain flowers
are yellow. No sound from the trees.
Not even birds.

Translations of the poetry of

DARIUSZ NISZEWSKI
(b. 1977 – d. 2015)

Very little is known about Dariusz Niszewski. He apparently
studied history and literature at the University of Warsaw,
though it's unclear whether he was enrolled in an official
capacity. In any event, following his time in Warsaw he showed
up in Poznań, where he became known for his talking, and
where he died prematurely in the summer of 2015. My friend,
Dawid Koloszyc, claims to have met him in the summer of 2013.
A few months after his death Niszewski sent Dawid his
collected poems, four of which are published in translation
here for the first time.

CREDO

Here the forest has an outer limit.

I have walked to a clearing within it,
beyond the orchard's arthritic clutch,

I have returned with a child's hair curled
in my right hand while the five fingers of my left

meld together like a small wing. I flap it
in a myth of one-handed flight. Not otherwise

than this do I refute the numbers of those heaped
in the barn that stood in my village, the barns

in the village next to my village, where in 1941
those who stood awkwardly in the cold walked

through the doors reserved for their horses,
and were summarily burned along with their horses,

cattle, pigs, small dogs, small children, hay.
From the next town over, others wait for new

arrivals in morning, the requisition of their grain,
watch the horizon flicker like a light-bulb burning out.

HISTORY

It is a species made entirely of very short men
whose stiff bowler hats here confirm the fact,

as seems likely, that none of them have arrived into
present circumstances with their faces.

What environmental pressure selected for the absence
of the face? How many years until finally the eyes,

or what were eyes, assumed the pallor and touch
of a newborn's skin? And where then the nose? Mouth?

Ears? Hold one of them down by the shoulders, pin
your knee into his gut, hammer your will against his will

and stare into his face: it is the white flesh of an almond.
I've watched them on their way, turning at once this direction

and that, occupying boulevards and congealing as if to rest,
and then turning once again so that what was as random

as leaves blowing soon revealed to me the wind's furtive design.
Tell me what is the end towards which their restless scuttling moves?

How many times must they circle the earth? In the night
I've heard a few going through the garbage like dirty raccoons.

Tell me where are the children now that they are near?
Who has left the children unattended? Go quickly, go.

MYTH

His entire strength is deficient
though he holds on with all his strength,

his inhuman heroic strength, sung into myth,
beheld in stories, slayer of monsters,

equal among the jealous gods; Protean
in his appetites and father of the children

of an entire nation, this idol of Odysseus,
his massive power, irrefutable as logic, proves

nothing against that element come so near us
from very far away; his shrinking hands pried open,

all the strength of his minuscule hands, sufficient
in his day to grip the outer edge of our horizon,

are now like the hands of a child, growing smaller,
groping into the space where his father's hands were.

HAPPINESS

How stupid you are, stupid girl! Who can blame you?
Not I! Not I! You're not as stupid as all that now,

are you? You didn't know what to do
with the tractor, you didn't know how to milk it,

sweet girl, you can barely stand up, your little feet
like the stumps of broken trees. You squat

as if to piss beside that broken machine (if it ever worked)
with a brassiere over your ears because you believe

it useful for warmth, and the father of the boy to whom
you promised your heart shot your father, and your brother

left home for a better life in the east, and your mother got lost
on her way to market, and home again (home again) you play

with the parts of the engine you can handle with your hands
and sing a song, a little prayer, to the Mother of Christ who heals

the dumb, turns oil into milk, who fastens happiness down with her latch.

II

This is the way the West is won
And why I run.

IN MEMORY OF MURRAY JOHNSON

[i]

I don't know what is that bitterness inside love
after which we trouble ourselves
because you had shown us nothing
more noble than poetry and the lives of poets

who died too young or too late or behaved terribly
to their daughters, going blind or running away
from their families, becoming drunks, the jazz
they listened to, how Charlie Mingus once challenged

a group of BC Lions linebackers at the bar to step outside—
they'd been talking, you see, while Mingus performed
his music. *Is there a better album than* Ah Um,
Mr. Johnson? No, I don't think there is, he warned,

as if to prepare us that loving art in this way meant
returning again because you'd failed the first time.
So Milton required of us a lifetime; Keats, the same;
Coleridge, who sank into his opium, laid his head down

and dreamt his masterpiece, mostly lost on waking...
It's all so lonely being so dead except for what's written,
the poems in your Norton, The Compact Edition
of the *Oxford English Dictionary* in two volumes

on your desk. Who bends his body so close to the script,
the scrap heap of words in columns as if there is a rule
to follow, as if any teacher ever knew how to proceed
after he'd given that gift of seeing what's hidden there,

hidden openly, except that now we've also been wounded
into the violence and luminous aftermath of the violence
of poetry. When I look up from my poems
at the mess on my desk I see so many magnified cities,

the wreckage of Lowell's life, the twentieth century collected
several times over—in Milosz, Auden, Akhmatova. You must
read "The Quaker Graveyard in Nantucket," it will ruin
your life if you take it seriously as it summons you

to its stanzas over again, reciting again, committing it all
to your memory's severed ice sheet; though you may
love your wife and children, though you may be a good
man, all I've shown you will ghost you, snaffle your days—

[ii]

Your students have to live with what was here
When you showed us how the old masters hid
In plain view the secrets of their art like a bid
At an auction in which there could be only a loser;
Where poems were evidence of having lost
A little less than total failure. It was almost cruel
To kindle in us an ambition that to others is all cost,
No reward, no plan to fall back upon
That wasn't fraught by poetry. You paced the classroom,
Row by row, brought to us a patience suited,
Perhaps, to exactly this—the sympathy of a master
Teacher for the brackish dreams of kids booted
Too soon or at exactly the right time into their lives,
And who step aside your shade on this day you died.

SELF-PORTRAIT

after Robert Lowell's version of Rilke

The bags under his eyes have the look
Of an oil spill, a snapshot
From space of black-blue continents.
A tired boy is tiptoe behind the eyes,
And there's a kind of weariness, not a cynic's
Decline, but an only child's still-life stare.
The mouth frowns when no one is looking,
Stiffens to a lizard baking in the sun.

And yet the forehead, the crevice of the brow,
Is already inclined otherwise, into the next year,
Already quick with change. Close by, his son
Quickens his life, breaks it into two plus one.

FOURTEEN WEEKS AT SEA

for Louis

How Odysseus swims for days

through troubled seas

cursed to be living,

fated by the Earth-Shaker to life, and fails

to drown, fails to sink under into the land of fish

and sea-gods — those whales, the great grey whale

who swallows the ocean and spits it up,

swallows and splurges it all again

and again, so that in this way the ocean continues to be —

until he is finally tossed up on a beach,

naked, without companions.

GIVEN A WEEK AND A NIGHT

You know the one, like a beggar at dawn,
who at street-level smiles and fawns,
hard luck, nothing left of his own to pawn?

That guy, face sunk into the head of a pint
but stirred to life near the end of each night—
what he'd do, greatly, if only he might?

And the women whose love he banked on?
I hear he'd a way of coming on too strong,
either that or his calculations went wrong.

Of children, it's true he fathered a few,
a couple of girls—or were there more than two?—
if he sees them once a year, that will do,

that will be enough, given his kind of man,
within whose body like a cripple he stands,
all his life like the love of a perpetual cover band.

If you've felt for him with any sympathy,
wondered what in his place you'd have done differently,
then we're not so far apart as I thought initially.

DOUBT AND FAITH

He might wonder all his life
whether his decisions were betrayals,
whether he found love out of fear,
what prompted him to stay,
what in him wished to leave.

Or how the ghost of a breath on the glass
is for the faithful a sign,
and what each sees is his own Christ,
his own Mary Mother of God in the glass.

And many years after
his children crouch low, as to a shrine.

So he might wonder
and saddle up his own part-starved steed,
pastured and bruised in a kiln-dried country

where he rides, tacking trails cut above the sea.
O what a lovely seaside view!
Desire like a mule's wish, declining its absolute.

WANDERING SOLUTIONS SEEK
HOSPITABLE PROBLEMS

Think of a woven fish trap plaited by the woman
Whose heart is pierced by a burrowed blue hole.
The fish thrash at the head of her wicker basket.
Think of an untidy mass of tentacles protruding
Into the ocean. Backs to the sea, nowhere to go.
Think of Diderot's disapproval of travel: civility
Is lived in cities; and beyond cities, mere cruelty.
I think the century has had enough of Europe.
Books amass on the floor of my back-room study
And I do not know where to begin. The woman
At my door arrived from the Mesolithic Danube,
A fish caught in her coral throat. A flap of skin
Flutters when she sings her throaty deep song.
Further east the land broadens and the one river
Splits backward into many tributaries; stranger,
This demographic is a fish trap: go westward, lunge.

THE HERMIT CRAB SCUTTLES ACROSS THE SAND FROM ONE SHELL TO A NEW AND MORE COMFORTABLE ONE

It wasn't that bad. Depending on which uniform
Banged at the door I'd say we'd always lived here
Or—*Who's asking?* There were no shortages
Of federalist visions; we had flexible identities.
In the cities rent was cheap. Someone's trash
Usually ended up at my house: I'd take bookshelves;
Then there was that old couch. Burckhardt wrote
Of our *unprecedented variety of life.* Masses rejoiced
In the profusion of the masses—my bread and butter.
I'm like the hermit crab who, in general, is never satisfied
With its current living conditions. Blames the tide
Or some beach party for its pissy desire to move again.
The danger is in the transitional phase, scuttling
In clear view across the sand, where gulls cock their grub,
Never at home. A broad consensus emerges hereafter—
Nothing to do with despotism. *Who's asking,*
Less important. Catastrophe periodically ensures that peace
Is merely the time given between wars, when the good,
Like a garage sale, is good for the getting.

THE CHRONIC FUTILITY OF INVENTION

for Warren Heiti

Despite superficial differences,
Conclusions almost identical
To those of Plato
Involved the assertion of an order
Declared irrational: a replica, a counterpart
To everything else belonging to the ephemeral:
The typical alone shone permanent. Thus envisioned,
Plato discerned a dusty trail where many horses once stampeded.
So he rode his own bare-knuckled steed
West where, betokened of calamity and parched, he waited
At the shore of the Atlantic Ocean. Seafaring rabble swarmed,
Democratic in effect if not intention: they haggled over prices. Plato
Poured libations over the sand, all the rest of his wine.
The wine wasn't his, actually. But that didn't matter.

REDUCED BY IMPLACABLE BOREDOM
TO THE LAST STAGES OF IDLENESS

I don't have it in me. I memorized
All the instructions. You bequeathed to me a map
And rules so clear and simple anyone could understand.
Forget horses. Here is an impersonal method
For discovering truths on a large, profitable scale.
Nothing more is operated by native power
Of land and water; you closed up the workshop.
But I'm impatient with difficult things. I've a narrow hope,
It is this: that the dry soul is neither wisest nor sickest.
I flee from my station into the fields and finally
Forests. I cross highways. I smoke that map
And stash one last flare into my bag before I depart:
I proceed thus-and-so through landscapes lost. And light my flare
At exactly the wrong time while bombers lumber steadily
Across the sky. That view from above is way above me.
Between the attunement of our judgments bombs
Clobber the otherwise quiescent and luminous dawn.
I read once I'm to wrestle at the limits of what's said,
But it's like I slept again through the alarm. Or screamed
In real-time when I screamed while I slept. I recalled
No sense of having really done so. I emerge awake
Again, get on with the day, either past the limit already
Or so far behind I'm stuck with the day job given to me.
If I had any choice at all I'd have advocated for an age
Of less proficiency. For the calendar year divided by Lent
And Advent seasons. Call me in from the queue. I'm spent.

THE INHUMAN DEMANDS OF PATRIOTISM

for Matt Rader

We may here observe a destiny: it is a cosmic
Logic men are at liberty to flout, if they choose,
And expose themselves to an inevitable penalty.
Aeneas remains in the arms of Dido: cheating
His western kingdom of both *west* and *kingdom*.
On the other hand, fortune must be borne to be
Overborne, or I'm bored silly. *Faber est quisque fortunae suae*:
An imaginative picture, it provides also a criterion
Of behaviour. Seen thus Dido was a starlet,
Subsequently to find her more adequate expression
In a city not built by human hands. These developments,
However, were reserved for a future
In which the cycle of *civitas terrena* should have
Worked itself out—but, sadly, did not.

A PLAY

for Robbie Moser

We'd arrive, if only we could get there.
If we could only rush there by arriving
I'd find a way to get away from my station,

to take my leave. Yet if I have already left,
taken off, and if I were not by now a long way off,
would I know you when I saw you, as if

you were a *you* and I someone eagerly on
my way? This is a setback, yes? Or is it a plentitude
like the stars from which I cannot mark a way

away? From cradle to cradle, from birth
to worse, unreported, I think, on the news,
I sought some mystery by way of my dreams,

turned up the first spade I ever really dug
into the dirt. The dirt is exactly what it seems
to be. A piece of earth, that goddess of gifts

and forgiveness. I could use one or the other.
I'll offer you one or the other, when I've gone.

IMPROVED EQUIPMENT

These are the mountains
I've stashed into
my improved equipment.
Look up, brother,
and tread across
their woolly tundra.
Where you hurdle
canyons I crack
the wind between
my teeth, spit turbulent
rivers up.
Salmon flee
birth, return
to die. If I die,
you'll know it
by my lacking one
or another of these
things: either wind
or the river. It'll be
a disappearing
act: fed up with sky,
there is no sky.
Fed up with oceans,
there is a dry
mouth gaping
at what-was-sky,
what-was-moon.

Climbing now the hills,
a clear view way
above startles us
awake: you
at last catch sight
of a massive buck,
who stands stunned
in a clearing and leaps
and clears the bone-time
of my hand. The more
deceived, the very last
one, waits in the water,
as always she does.
If you find her, say this.

A NOTE TO VIRGIL IN THE UNDERWORLD

Who would have guessed Hades included the streets
we knew in Montreal? The bakery is boarded up,
but the sidewalks are still dirty. I suspect the neighbours
are home but it's hard to be sure in winter. No matter,
we hardly saw anyone until spring and by then
their children were suddenly teenagers.
Perhaps they've all gone away by now—everyone.
It's hard to be sure. If I walk a little too far
I approach the border of another city I do not know,
another city full of furies. The noise is overwhelming.
So I wait in the Montreal part of the underworld,
back in our apartment, which looks a lot like we left it
before packing up the books and dressers.
Before, that is, we left for good. I'd not have guessed
this return. But when you come looking for me,
you'll probably check here, so I'll wait as long as it takes.
Your bedroom is exactly as it was—a crib and spare bed,
a few paintings from daycare. There's the living room couch.
A few plates and a frying pan in the kitchen. A bit
of coffee in the coffee jar. My study seems as cluttered
with books as ever. The rumour is you've discovered a leak
in that image you've sustained of your father, the one with which
you argue, struggle, love. Colours drain from its face; lips
thinning; skin turning translucent. I didn't mean to leave you
with my shade only, its parroting of the few things I said
and did again and again. Always drinking a beer,
always tossing you up onto the pillows of the couch.

I'm here because this is where you first found me
like unpacked luggage after a long trip when you finally
arrived into your life. It's where you in turn stashed
what of me you could carry. (I'd squirrelled away
my shame and failures but I'm sorry to say
they're still here where I left them.) I suppose your mother
will wonder where you've gone and I hope you'll not worry her.
No doubt you'll find your way back home. The sunlight here
is adequate, if not authentic. The days do their best imitation
of real days. Each night, I've noticed, is moonless.
I'm always in the mood for wine when the snow falls.
Still, I'd say it's more like early March,
when false spring comes. Everyone in the city
knows it won't last but how we so adore it.
Listen: what I can give you now is already gone
but there are words left and I promise I'll tell you
exactly how we were and how it was in our life then.

POEM BEGINNING WITH A LINE
BY MICHAEL DONAGHY

They might have sung where we've no skill to reckon,
At the outpost where soldiers face an ocean.
Close by, the corporal monitors the sonar
And to his left another sets the charge.

Above, the moon gives light to what I write,
To my love, my sweet, my darling wife. Quiet
Still except for the sea, but the sea is not a song.
It is peace beyond which we've no skill to reckon.

This final hour before dawn they sing again,
And the crew fails to plug our ears for long.
I stall for time, and stall because it is too late.
They've sung where we've no skill to reckon.

CARTWRIGHT MOUNTAIN

All the loons on a lake that badly mitigates its new life
as a tailings pond, water the colour of a bad night
on mushrooms: nostalgia. Anger the size
of a barn. Rage like a garbage dump.
Heartbreak, a ponderosa pine,
tinder-stick dry. Coming of Age, a long drive
to nowhere so that when the car pulls into
Wynyard it's easier to remember
what it felt like later to drive away shit-smeared
with a dog. Left alone, I mean,
Solitude, a long road beside an orchard at night.
The sprinklers spraying water above all the mangled
apple trees. It's peaceful there. Nothing is dead.
Being next to nothing, absolutely so, is exactly like that.

OUR SPECIAL REPORT

Now that the summer is here the Arctic's
Crowded: phytoplankton bloom
While fish, birds, and whales are gorging.
Migratory geese breed in the North
And perform new Arctic rituals: this is
No anomaly; the polar pack shrivels
Like a salted slug. The land thaws
And some species will probably die out.
The nineteenth-century clearance sale
On North American forests pertained only
To trees. As our special report will demonstrate,
The world, mad, ignoring causes for market
Effects, engineers general calamity. Permafrost halos
High summer and retreats, shrinks, shirks its last stand,
A loser. Fair weather's immediately ahead.

HABITABLE EARTH IN LAST ANALYSIS

It's like in a cartoon, all the forest fires
Leapfrogging fires. Small civilizations caught
In the dirty say they're sorry and plead their cases
Ad hoc and brilliantly. *Scared as shit*
Is my summary. Excuses get you
An extra minute. The army is always
Dragging the mutilated
Corpses of the newest emperor
And his son through the streets. It's no wonder
The sky is filled with frogs. Upturned,
The ocean spills its fish and seashells and sharks.
In the old country you could count on fine weather
All summer, vernal festivals, voluptuary laws
That sanctioned the General Course of Things.
It was a pleasure then, being alive
When a fifth of the world was known. The downturn
Happens when the knowing is over. It's like
A forgetfulness comes on, a bad cold
That you didn't know you had until recovery
Commenced. By then, though, you're dead,
And so it's the afterlife playing its cards and tricks.
You recall the old neighbours, how they packed
Shoeboxes of photographs. And that cartoon again,
When the talking animals all flee the forest,
Tailed by a great deluge of fire and wind. As if running
Could get you to the somewhere else it's better to be at.
The great romance was this: there'd always be somewhere to go.
Otherwise there is no literature. As for me, I grabbed a novel
Though I'd never found time for fiction. It's science fiction now,
Says the Judger. I told you so, says the river, which by now is everything.

ON THE ORIGINS OF THINGS

for Nate Moser

The day you were born astronomers squinted past
The sky, charted unfixed stars and solar systems
Bearing the trace of their origins like stitches of ancestry
Woven into what they are. It's possible to determine
How long ago the Big Bang occurred, marking
The time when time began and what-is burst nothing
Back into non-being and life curled in its gaseous womb;
Then a billion years of fiery planets and icy moons,
And a mostly uninhabitable cosmos, so that no gambler
Would bet on anything like any of us happening at all:
How at 9:01 a.m. in the month of February, close to the end
Of an especially cold winter, it'll be told in the record books
That a huge asteroid clipped past our planet—a near miss.
We squeezed our breath and life swooped into your lungs.

BIRTHDAY LETTER

for Ian Orti

[i]

Ian,

You know November in Montreal.
It's like that now, exactly: cold and clear,
sun up, bare trees, leaves everywhere. All in all

it's easy to walk around so long as you prepare
for sudden shifts in weather, quick turns
in temperature. Ice-rain, sleet, snow: each shares

our fates. Today is the end of my thirty-fourth term
on earth, my birthday. This is my birthday poem!
It's an annual ritual, how I mark the debt earned

by being here, kicked, like you, by confusion.
The same creditors hound our middle age:
the problem, e.g., of desire, won't flee: the loan

it sharks is us. Is this, though, a new stage?
Do years follow one after another
or are they built together the way words on a page

form a story and show a life better
than each discarded moment? Wait. You've no time
for *high-flown bullshit*—I'd do best to remember

that for you decorum involves mostly what we mime
with our lives but don't pretend to speak or know.
But maybe you snip your tongue too often and too fine,

so that we listen as over an old rotary phone
to a party line and the voices are muffled,
almost background static but still obviously human.

It's easy to break a rhyme, to complain we're shackled
by the constraint of repetition. Each day, we fear,
is a drab repeat and drudge, consecutive but diminished.

(In this way you fear the aged locals at the bar
in the middle of the afternoon, drunk by six o'clock,
because one responds to your name. You're sure,

for a very weird second, that he's you and drop
by accident your pen in your beer). Ten years ago
I feared—still now the same fear—the graceless stop,

stuck in the rut of an uneven rage, the muted blow
of having forgone that risk Socrates urges us to take:
to be the world's fool and seek what we don't know.

We never talked, though, about Plato, whom I read
years before we became friends. November,
late fall, turns me onto Platonic moods. That we're fed

other than by bread alone is a faith I got somewhere,
now lodged in me like a nursery rhyme among
so much daily news from the *Globe* and the *Star*.

What am I to make of it there? From that cave flung
into daylight, Plato had his hero stumbling around blind
until his eyes adjusted to that brightness, where birds sang

and he was all alone, uneasy in the wind.
Maybe it's a place to which he's gone, maybe it's his room
after dinner or early in the morning when the hours find

him unoccupied with trades and chores and things to do.
For the clear view from above is not forever, I suspect.
I suspect we are alone in sudden visions. However true

they are, we return to the kitchen. How not to defect
either to one side or the other but strike an edge
in the distance between the two — and reject

neither transcendence nor the daily drudge? The ledger
I imagine we keep is parsed in hours and according to year.
The question ages like Scotch. You'll uncork it, a pledge

to your daughter and the woman she'll one day appear
to be as if all at once. You'll love her with a fear
so great it'll define the exact outline of your life.

[ii]

You'd probably not guess as you're reading this
but I've taken this poem to the Bagel Etc. for breakfast
and I'm sitting over hot black coffee—it's a bliss

that'd garner no great admiration from a saint
or from those who leave cities to walk among mountains,
living rugged and away. What way of life is best,

I don't know, but I think the question remains,
that we're rudderless if we don't ask it. School
often missed our real need. Books weren't to blame

if they were jimmied into hypotheses and material
for exegesis. Books meant always otherwise:
sudden love and up all night till dawn, entirely physical

your attraction to the first woman whose eyes
you mapped and skin you smelt like rank leaves,
a sort of rot to your innocence. You loved and despised

at once and learned what you knew of flesh, believing
in impulse, a real pain in the heart, then so many years
of desire like whiplash after a crash—until finally fucking,

utterly disappointed. Maybe one day you go for a beer
with that girl you knew. Maybe you meet her at a dive
on Johnson Street. And that's the last you see of her.

What then shall we say of Romanticism and its prize
—what? Epiphany? Life made more abundant? Or kicks
repeated and city and city and city and city,

never standing still? Now you've a child in the mix,
and her mother, whom you barely knew before conceiving.
I married. Our early-twenties Doubles would be sick,

daring or imploring us not to redo the cycle of becoming,
all this unrecognized by their ideal expectations.
But what refuted what? Your kidney overcoming

you for most of a year, you pissed blood—some vision!
I lost my appendix suddenly last summer,
close to bursting. I wheeled around the institution

and received pity from patients much sicker
than myself. I might have died, or you. We've joked
about what we'll say at each other's

funerals, what song will best sing either of us when we croak,
(a dumb rhyme, I know). I mean mortality
matters; it works on us as meaning works in poems—

not the time part but the way a whole season,
its cold or heat, handles everything at once. Calendar
dates, like my stack of *The Economist,* hidden

out-of-sight in a pile, one year then another
accumulate. So if I stash my youth into a single day?
Or the few years I've loved as if into a decade so dear

I cannot see behind it or beyond? How to stay
in a single place, to live as if it were home,
with a love not nomadic? Even the attempt to say

this much must try your patience. I won't crow
for too much longer. At thirty-five I'm taking a shot
at early mid-life reckoning, with no Hermes to show

the way further on. Unlike the kid I was, I'm caught
by what I've pocketed of love; hence the mystery.
This autumn, for instance, I've listened mostly to Bach,

especially his Partita #2 in C minor. It strikes me
that the question I've asked, about how we should be,
which life is better, ought to be thought of as polyphony,

one desire counterpointing others. Probably
I've said too much, or not enough, both inadequately,
a hell of a theme for a poet. So enough already.

It's getting late. Iris is drinking wine at a work party.
She just called. In the old days I'd be calling you
to grab a pint at the Precinct. Which reminds me.

AFTERWORD

Very little is known about Darren Bifford. He apparently studied philosophy at the University of Victoria, though it's unclear whether he was enrolled in an official capacity. In any event, following his time in Victoria, he showed up in Halifax, and eventually in Montreal, where he became known to a few local writers, eventually settling in a small apartment with a wife and child or children. In the summer of 2017 he headed west. He was last seen disappearing up scree slopes on mule-back, tacking trails cut above the sea: "O what a lovely seaside view! / Desire like a mule's wish, declining its absolute."

What is the world of *False Spring?* In "The Scene from Here" we are given a kind of establishing shot, a view of a home place ("my mother's patio") where things are going awry. The weather is inclement, the air the speaker breathes is dry. "The mountain flowers are yellow," he says. "No sound from the trees. / Not even birds."

In vernacular terms, this is a vision of a silent spring: but is it a true vision of a "false spring"? Or a false vision of a true spring? Does it come to us from the Gate of Ivory or the Gate of Horn?

In mythological terms, it is a vision of Hellmouth, Avernus, the Virgilian lake where no birds sing. It is the foyer of the underworld, the beginning of a catabatic journey.

The Cumaean Sibyl hangs out on the shores of Avernus. Like me she is a scholar, albeit of questionable practices. They say that in her youth she rebuffed the advances of a god, and so he cursed her with eternal life uncoupled from eternal youth: she became older and older, until she was a husk inside a bottle, suspended from the branches of a tree. Her prophesies were confused statements, fragmentary, whirling leaves. What do you suppose she said?

The end arrives exactly when you're looking.
Stay here until you learn a new song.
The dirt is exactly what it seems to be.
Keep your eyes on the children.
It is easy to descend Avernus, but to find your way back—hoc opus, hic labor est.

AMANDA JERNIGAN
Hamilton, Ontario, 2017

64

"The Inhuman Demands of Patriotism" and "The Characteristic Futility of Invention" borrow from Charles Norris Cochrane's *Christianity and Classical Culture.*

"Reduced by Implacable Boredom to the Last Stages of Idleness" cribs a few expressions from Descartes, Kant, and Wittgenstein.

"On the Origin of Utopias" lifts the first sentence and a few words of the second from Edmund Phelps' essay *What Is Wrong with the West's Economies*, printed in NYRB vol. LXII, number 13.

"Wandering Solutions Seek Hospitable Problems" also takes a few expressions from an essay in the NYRB, but I cannot recall what issue or essay except that it would have been in published in 2012.

The first line of the second part of "In Memory of Murray Johnson" borrows the first line of the first sonnet of Robert Lowell's *History.*

"This Sunset Lasts Forever" borrows one line each from W.H. Auden, Mary Jo Bang, and Ezra Pound.

"Our Special Report" steals a few lines from *The Economist*, though I can't recall from what issue.

"Of First and Last Things" borrows its title and theme from the first section of Nietzsche's *Human, All Too Human.*

ACKNOWLEDGEMENTS

These poems were written and published with the generous support of the Canada Council for the Arts and Conseil des arts et des letters du Québec.

Some of these poems were published in *Hermit Crab,* a limited edition from Baseline Press in 2014 and as *The Age of Revolution,* Anstruther Press, 2017. Thanks to Karen Schindler and Jim Johnstone, respectively.

"Birthday Letter" was published in *Event* and excerpted in *McSweeney's.* "Wandering Solutions Seek Hospitable Problems" was published in *The Lonely Offices.* "The Hermit Crab Scuttles across the Sand from One Shell to a New and More Comfortable One" was published in *Hazlitt.* "Doubt and Faith" was published in *The Walrus.* "A Play" and "Reduced by Implacable Boredom to the Last Stages of Idleness" were published in *Matrix.* "Failure of the International System" and "While Great Nations Recast Greater Nations Rush In" were published in *The Winnipeg Review.* "Habitable Earth in Last Analysis" and "Stay" were published in *This Magazine.* "The Elements of Cohesion Must Be Weakened," "Archaic Torso," "On Tyranny," and "The View from Here" were published in *Numero Cinq.* "The Birth of Revolutionary Desire," "Of First and Last Things," and "False Spring Is the New Thing" were published in *The Fiddlehead.*

Thanks to the editors of these magazines. Thanks to my friends who read and commented on many of these poems, especially Alayna Munce and Amanda Jernigan. Thanks to Don McKay for the letters and phone calls.

DARREN BIFFORD is the author of *Wedding in Fire Country* (Nightwood Editions, 2012) and *False Spring* (Brick Books, 2018), as well as the chapbooks *Wolf Hunter* (Cactus Press, 2010), *Hermit Crab* (Baseline Press, 2014), and *The Age of Revolution* (Anstruther Press, 2017). He lives in Montreal.